*Books by the author:*

# THE
# CAMELS
*Ships of the Desert*

# THE CAMELS

## Ships of the Desert

GEORGE LAYCOCK
With photographs by the author

Doubleday & Company, Inc., Garden City, New York

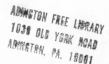

*Library of Congress Cataloging in Publication Data*
*Laycock, George*
*The camels: ships of the desert.*
*Summary: Briefly describes the characteristics of*
*the camel and its relationship to man throughout history.*
*1. Camels—Juvenile literature. [1. Camels]*
*I. Title.*
*QL737.U54L39        599'.736*
*ISBN 0-385-07137-X   Trade*
*0-385-09531-7   Prebound*
*Library of Congress Catalog Card Number 73–13090*

# THE
# CAMELS
*Ships of the Desert*

When I awakened in the early morning there were big feet padding through the camp. The sun was rising and a strange lumpy shape cast a shadow on the side of my tent. I climbed out of bed for a good look at this animal.

Standing under the acacia tree was a giant camel.

We had come to Africa to ride the camels into the desert and take pictures of wild animals. I looked at the camel again. Did I really want to ride him after all?

Like most other camels I had seen, he was not very pretty, he was about the same color as the dust in which he stood. His legs were long and knobby. His neck was thick and crooked. He had a long, narrow

*Knobby-kneed, big-footed, and hump-backed, the camel is a strange, lumpy animal with a long and noble history.*

*One of them had a rope around her neck and from it hung
a wooden bell that gave soft, sweet tones as she swung along.*

face that was small for such a large animal and he was looking back at me from half-closed eyes as if he dared me to come on out of my tent and try to ride him.

At the same time, he was trying to swat the flies that buzzed around him. But he had a ridiculous little tail too short to reach anything but a very careless fly. He had a big hump on his back. His body was large and very high above the ground, as if he stood on stilts.

Then more camels came plodding into camp. One of them had a rope around her neck and from it hung a wooden camel bell that gave soft sweet tones as she swung along. Behind the camels came the drivers carrying their spears and speaking softly among themselves. They worked every day with these strange animals. On this day they were supposed to show us how to ride them.

Camels, for thousands of years, have walked the hot desert sands carrying people and freight. Because of camels, men have lived and worked in deserts where they would not have been able to live at all without these remarkable animals.

This strange animal, called the "ship of the desert," has done far more than carry people and their belongings.

Camels have carried soldiers into battle. They are still used by soldiers on desert patrol. In North Africa I met three game wardens riding on camels. They were protecting the elephants, giraffes, and other wild animals from poachers. Camels also have been used to carry mail, even in the United States.

Imagine one thousand camels spread out in a line and loaded with salt, silk, and tea. Once, long ago, such caravans were sent westward out of Peking, China, to cross the mountains on trips that sometimes lasted for two months.

They have even been used as money. A man's camels are a sign of his wealth. In the way some people save money, a camel owner may try to keep all the camels he can get. In ancient times ten camels would buy a man a fine wife. Then, if he had some camels left they would provide milk for drinking and for making cheese. Women even used camel's milk for face cream. They claimed it made their skin soft and smooth. Even the camel dung is used; it is dried and burned for fuel.

It is no wonder that there are no wild camels left in Asia and Africa. All of the camels belong to someone.

Visitors from foreign countries often think it would be fun to ride camels. Some camels do nothing except haul tourists. Their owners hire them out for taxi duty.

12

*Wild camels are gone. All camels belong to someone and a man's beasts are his wealth.*

*Since ancient times long lines of camels have walked the dr*

ands, carrying man's riches on their humped backs.

One day in Cairo, Egypt, the camel drivers were given some bad news. The city officials told them they could no longer charge the tourists so much money to ride their camels around the Great Sphinx and the pyramids. They were even told they would have to stop taking tips. In addition they would have to get new camel licenses every year.

All this made the camel drivers extremely unhappy. They talked it over with their leader, a sixty-one-year-old camel owner named Lamel Ghoneim. Voices grew loud and arms waved in the air. The camel drivers simply would not stand for this interfering in their business. Lamel Ghoneim said, "Maybe we should go on strike. Not let our camels work at all. Then what will the tourists do for camels to ride?"

Angrily, Mr. Ghoneim led his camel home. He took off the camel's saddle and turned the camel out to rest. Then he sat down to think. All the other camel drivers followed his example. That day no camels walked around the Great Sphinx and the pyramids with tourists on their backs. No tourists had their pictures taken on camels. The whole thing was very sad. Everyone wished the camels would come back.

Finally, after six days, the officials changed their minds. They told Lamel Ghoneim that the camel owners could return. They would not have to lower their prices after all.

This made the camel drivers happy again. They rode their camels back to work. Then to celebrate their victory they all trotted their camels around the Great Sphinx and the pyramids. That made a fine parade, one hundred and forty camels and their riders. The tourists were so glad to see the camels again that they applauded the camel drivers in their victory ride.

Even the camels seemed contented. Why not? They had just enjoyed a six-day rest.

Most of the time camels and airplanes do not get into each other's way. But one day some years ago a camel in Cairo, Egypt, wandered out to the international airport. Up in the control tower the workers did not notice the brown beast walking along the edge of the airport. They were busy listening to pilots calling on the radio for landing and take-off instructions. Big airplanes and little airplanes came and went. Jets roared off the long paved airstrip leaving broad black smoke trails behind them and hauling people to new adventures around the world.

This did not bother the camel. He strolled along as if he did not know where he was and did not really care. Finally he walked out toward one of the runways.

At the other end of the runway sat a gigantic jet plane, a Boeing 707. Its engines were running beautifully. The passengers were strapped in their seats. The

17

crew in the nose of the big jet liner was busy checking out all the instruments for the take-off.

Up in the control tower the traffic directors still had not noticed the big brown camel. They told the pilot of the jet that he was cleared for take-off. The jet started down the runway and began gaining speed.

The camel did not pay much attention to the big machine coming on collision course toward him. He walked calmly down the middle of the runway.

At the last moment the pilot looked out and saw the camel in his path. There was no hope of getting the plane off the ground soon enough to fly over the animal. The camel did not give the plane the right-of-way.

There was nothing else the pilot could do but run the jet liner off into the grass. He sat there shaking and thinking about the close call.

What did the camel do? He only walked on down the runway as if nothing had happened. The control tower stopped all airplane traffic, a dozen guards rushed onto the field, finally caught the lost camel and led him away.

Most of us live so far from camel country that we only see camels in the zoo. Even zoo keepers know their camels can cause trouble and they must not let visitors and camels get too close together. In one zoo a camel that had always been friendly suddenly leaned far out of its pen and grabbed a girl's hair in its teeth. At first the girl thought the camel was playing. But the camel pulled her hair out and she knew better. After that she never liked camels much.

It could have been worse. In Lima, Peru, some years ago a zoo visitor stayed until evening. He had been drinking alcoholic beverages and was not quite certain where he was. But he knew he was tired and wanted to sleep. He opened a big iron door and went inside, planning to lie down for a night's rest. But the pen already was occupied by a big camel that did not want a roommate. The camel became so infuriated that it began biting the man, and hurt him so badly that he died on the way to the hospital.

Another zoo camel that became famous lived in the Oklahoma City Zoo. Her name was India and her speciality was predicting rain.

There had been no rain for several weeks. The countryside seemed dry as a desert. Every day the people on the streets and at the Weather Bureau looked into the skies hoping to see clouds that would bring rain to the city. But each new day dawned bright and clear.

Then one afternoon the camel's keeper saw India walk up onto a little hill in her enclosure. The camel stood there tall and straight. She lifted her face toward

19

the sky. She sniffed the air. Several times she did this. This could mean only one thing to the camel's keeper. He hurried to the zoo office. "There's going to be rain," he announced happily. "India predicted it. She went up and sniffed the air and that always means she smells rain."

The zoo called the Weather Bureau downtown. The weatherman smiled and shook his head. "So the camel says there is going to be rain? Maybe a camel should run my office." He looked out the window and the sky was clear. Not a trace of a cloud. He sniffed the air. Nothing. He studied his maps. No rain in prospect. He checked all the instruments weathermen usually check. No question about it, the camel was wrong. His prediction that day was "warm and continued clear."

But the next morning India was splashing happily about her pen and everywhere in town people talked about the cloudburst that came in the night.

Camels come in two styles. You can tell the two kinds apart by the number of humps on their backs. One is the Arabian camel and it has only one hump. These live in Arabia, India, and North Africa.

The other camel, the one with two humps, is the Bactrian and its home country is the Gobi Desert of northeastern Asia. The Bactrian has shorter legs and

*When work is done the weary Arabian camel rests on folded legs, and dreams, perhaps, of cool water and tender green salads.*

longer wool than the one-humped camel. The Gobi Desert, which has no trees and is twice as large as Montana, can be very hot in summer and bitterly cold in winter. The Bactrian camel, with its long hair, is ready for either kind of weather. It is also equipped with stronger, more rugged feet. This is important because instead of having sand to walk on, the Bactrian camels live in rough and rocky parts of the world.

Sometimes people talk about another kind of camel, the "dromedary." But the dromedary is really a special racing model of the one-humped camel. They are bigger than the average Arabian one-humped camel and they can walk faster. These are the riding camels.

There are about four million camels in the world. One million of them are Bactrian, the other three million are the one-humped Arabian camels.

The camel's family history goes back millions of years to a time when the world was much different from today. And strangely, the camel story leads back to North America. First there was a small, humpless camel on this continent. About forty million years ago, there also roamed here a giant camel that stood fifteen feet high. North American animals were the ancestors of modern camels. They are believed to have spread out in two directions. One branch of the family gradually moved southward and ended up in South

America. The llama is a modern cousin of the camel. The llama, which has no hump, is much smaller than the camel. Llamas stand about four or five feet high at the shoulders. But, like camels, they are used for meat, wool, and carrying burdens. And like camels, they have bad dispositions and do not always get along well with their owners.

Another branch of the camel family moved northwestward, toward Alaska. Scientists believe that a belt of land once connected North America and Asia. Along this land bridge animals extended their range in both directions. Some were coming toward North America. With them came the first people to arrive on the continent, the ancestors of the Indians, Aleuts, and Eskimos.

But the camels crossing over the land bridge appear to have been going in the opposite direction, west instead of east. They spread to Asia and Africa. They later died out in North America.

Time and the forces of nature have since shaped the camel to desert life. Most desert mammals survive by finding shade in the heat of the day, or by going underground in their burrows. But the camel must stay out in the sun. Scientists have studied the camel carefully to find out how it can live where many other animals would die. They have found some strange answers. It is well-designed for its life in the hot, dry, sandy parts of the world.

23

*The hot sands of a dry river bec*

*ecome a highway for the heavily loaded camels.*

Those longs legs may help it in more than walking. The hottest part of the desert is right at ground level. Up on those long legs, away from the scorching hot sands, the temperature is somewhat cooler for the camel's body.

Many people have looked at the hump on the camel's back and said, "Ah, there is the answer. The beast simply packs extra water in that hump on its back." But they are wrong about that because the camel's hump is not a big leather bag filled with surplus water. Instead the camel's hump is filled with fat. There may be eighty pounds or more of fat carried in the hump depending on the camel's size.

What would a camel's body do with all that fat? The fat is extra fuel. It provides energy to keep the camel going when times are bad and there is not enough food for it to eat. Then, the fat begins to disappear as the animal's body uses it. If the hard times last long enough, the camel's hump almost disappears. Owners can tell by the hump if the animal is in good enough condition to make a long journey.

In addition, the camel does a better job than most animals of saving water in its body. It does this in strange and remarkable ways. We keep cool on a hot day because water evaporates from our skins through sweat glands. This moisture carries heat away from our bodies. On a very hot day, we drink a lot of water

26

because sweating uses it up to keep our bodies cool. The camel, however, even in the hottest places in the world, gets along fine without doing much sweating at all. It does have sweat glands, a lot of them. But they do not have much work to do. Camel owners almost never see their camels sweat.

This puzzled scientists for many years. They knew that most mammals, including people, must keep their body temperatures about the same all through their lives. If a person's body temperature goes up, it is because he is sick and has a fever. But if the air temperature around us were to go up, and our body temperature could rise without hurting us, we would not have to sweat so much to keep cool because the outside heat would be closer to our own temperature. Then we would not have to drink so much water.

This is exactly what happens to the camel. Its body temperature, instead of being the same all the time, can change. As the weather becomes hotter, a camel's body temperature goes up as much as eleven degrees. The camel stays as comfortable as ever, and the water it would need to cool its body is saved.

Even when it does sweat a little bit, the moisture is held in that thick blanket of hair that covers its big lumpy body. This way the moisture helps cool the animal longer than it would if it could quickly evaporate into the air.

*The young camel, even before it must carry a load on its back, tags along and learns what it is like to walk all day.*

These are the reasons a camel can go so long between drinks and why it is the best of all animals for desert work. While camels are still young, their owners try to train them to go without water except maybe once every two or three days. If the weather is cool and there is sometimes _dew and rain on the plants, the camel may be three months or longer without a drink of water.

Besides, scientists now know that the camel can lose up to 40 per cent of its body moisture and still be healthy. Most mammals would die after the body gives off half as much, or 20 per cent, of its moisture.

But camels still know when they are getting thirsty. They will sometimes break into a run when they come close to an oasis. At the oasis the camel really makes up for going without water. One camel drank thirty gallons of water in ten minutes.

How long a camel can live, or travel, without water depends on several things over which the camel has no control. Strong sunlight, hot winds, and how much moisture is in the camel's food all make a difference. So does the weight it must carry, the distance it must walk, and the speed it must travel. Like the rest of us, the harder the camel works the more moisture it must have. But when times are dry and the going rough, the camel is still out there plodding along, because it is one of the world's best water conservationists.

The camels' pace is not a swift one. They can keep up a speed of about two and a half miles an hour when traveling in caravan. But they walk at the same speed hour after hour. By day's end the silent, hump-backed, brown animals moving in a line across the brown desert may travel eighteen to twenty miles. And each camel probably carried five hundred or six hundred pounds, sometimes more.

A good riding camel, traveling alone, can average five miles an hour. There is a record of one that walked fifty miles in a day. But thirty miles is a good day's travel, even for the best of camels.

If you look a camel in the face, you may notice that it has big droopy eyelids. Its eyelashes are long and beautiful. They help shade its eyes from the brilliant desert sun. When the wind blows sand into a camel's face the animal can close its nostrils with special shut-off valves. During sand storms the camel falls to its knees and closes its eyes. Then it stretches its long neck out flat against the earth and waits for the storm to pass.

On its knees and chest the camel has tough leathery pads. These help protect its body when kneeling.

Besides it has feet that are especially good for desert walking. It has two toes and the bones of its feet are wrapped in a leather pouch that seems a little big for a good fit. The feet can spread out somewhat and help to support the camel's weight on soft sand.

*No man can know what thoughts hide in that knobby head.*

*The oasis is the center of desert life, where the thirsty came*

*While camels drink gallon on gallon of water, the*

*nd their thirsty owners come to drink.*

*bear-carrying owners sit in a tight circle visiting with friends.*

*The broad feet of the camel spread its weight and keep it from sinking deeply into the sand.*

*Where the camels pass, they leave shallow footprints in the sand.*

*Thorny twigs are candy to a working camel free of its burden
at the end of the day.*

Most mammals would starve on what the camel gets to eat. Nothing seems too tough for it. In our camp in Africa when the hungry camels were turned out to eat after a long day's march, they would head straight for the thorn bushes. Twigs of these desert plants are covered with rows of tough hooked thorns. These thorns catch a person's clothes as he passes and tear holes in them. They hang on so tight that people call them "wait-a-bit thorns." But they are candy to a camel. The camel catches a branch of the thorn tree in its mouth and swings its head sideways, stripping off leaves, thorns and all. Then it munches happily, swallows, and reaches for more. Camels sometimes chew on leather or drink salty water without getting a stomach ache.

The camel may live to be forty years old. It is not an adult until it is about ten to twelve years old. After mating, the female camel must go eleven months before having her calf. From its earliest days the baby camel's legs are almost as long as its mother's. Even as an infant it stands far above the scorching sands. Otherwise it looks like a little copy of its parents.

Baby camels may not be able to keep up with their mothers on the long marches. What does the camel driver do? He can not leave the baby behind. Even if he wanted to, the mother camel would have none of that! Mother camels take very good care of their young ones. So when the camp must move, the smallest calves are loaded onto their mothers' backs. There they ride with blankets and other equipment, bumping up and down. Up there they can look out at the desert and see over the heads of all the other camels.

I found out what these baby camels see up there. It happened first on the day the camels plodded into camp and awakened me, the first day I ever rode a camel.

The first job was putting a saddle on my big camel. Camels are so tall they have to lie down before they can be saddled.

Gamia, my camel, had a rope looped around her lower jaw. Hasim, the camel driver, jerked on the rope and yelled something that sounded like "took." But the camel did not want to "took." She began jumping around and trying to stay away from Hasim. She knew what Hasim was up to. It was the same every day. Finally, however, the big camel knelt. Then the drivers fastened a saddle around her. She stood up and waited until the other camels were ready.

This was also the day the camel drivers decided to teach a young camel to carry its first load on a march. The camel was old enough to take his place in the long line of camels trudging over the sands. But the young camel did not want to learn his job. Four men were trying to fix a pack on his back and all of them were leaping about so that men and camels kicked up a dust storm. Each camel driver had a

*Long legs and humped back, the baby camel is a little copy of its parents.*

*Mother and daughter, all smiles for the photographer, show a strong family resemblance.*

rope, and each rope was tied to some part of the young camel.

The men were all yanking on the ropes and yelling. They were running around the young camel and switching its legs. Wack! Slap! Grunt! Snort! Bite! Kick! Jump! Wack! Slap! And slap again.

Finally the angry camel was lying down and holding still. Two of the men held their ropes very tight. The other two started to put the wooden frame on its back. Ropes had to be tied beneath the camel to hold the pack frame and the camel did not like this. Perhaps the young camel knew what a camel was supposed to do. Had he not seen the older camels being loaded every morning? Had he not heard their grumbling and moaning? Had he not seen them try to bite their masters? He tried all of these things too. But nothing would save him, and finally he stood silent and glaring beneath his pack.

Hasim, the camel driver, once more checked the big soft leather saddle on Gamia, my camel. Then it was time for me to get on her back. Gamia turned her head and tried to nip Hasim. But Hasim took off his hat and swatted Gamia across the face. Nobody likes to be slapped in the face by a dirty old hat, especially Gamia, the proud riding camel. I do not know whether kind words would have worked better. Would camels be nicer to people if we loved them more?

*Camels are so high they must lie down to be loaded. The*

*noan and groan, and bite if they can.*

*The working camel has a rope around its lower jaw. As it is loaded for the day's journey, it complains in camel language to its owner.*

*The camel was old enough to take his place in the long line of camels trudging over the sands.*

*When loading a camel, one must remember where its head is
because it will turn and bite if one forgets.*

But pretty soon Gamia grew tired of complaining, and began to lie down. Hasim turned to me with a big smile. I leaped to the saddle before Gamia had time to swing around and try to bite me. I pushed my feet out in front of me in the stirrups and braced myself. This kept me from sliding downhill toward her head when she stood up on her hind feet first. The front end of a camel is the first to go down and the last to come up. I found myself being lifted high above the desert. We moved off in the line. The camels stopped their grumbling. Everyone settled down for the march.

When a camel walks, it moves its two left feet forward at the same time. Then its two right feet move forward to catch up. This makes the animal seem to roll from side to side like a ship caught in the waves.

But I began to feel safe. The saddle was soft and my feet rested in the stirrups. In earlier times camel riders did not use stirrups. Instead they went bare-footed. That way they could catch some of the hair of the camel's neck in between their toes and use their feet to help hang on. They could also push against the camel's neck with their feet to help guide it.

Some people claim that camels do not really get lost, that they can always find their way over the desert and lead their masters home. But owners of camels know better than this. A camel may stop to feed and let the rest of the herd move on out of sight. Finally the camel looks up. He is alone! This makes him nervous. He moans in a low rumbling voice and trots off searching for his herd.

That night the camel owner counts his camels. One is gone! He goes searching for it. And while he searches, he sings his special camel song. His camels know their master's song and if the lost camel has followed some strange camels into another camp, and hears the song, he may come back to his own master.

In spite of all that camels have done for people through the ages, people have not been very kind to camels. Some men even keep camels for fighting so they can bet on which camel will kill the other one. Many kinds of animals have been kept for fighting. Bull fights are very popular in some places. Dogs have been fought against each other. So have roosters. Such animal fights are against the law in most places. There are also laws against putting two camels together to fight. But sometimes it is done anyhow. If you were to be in a little country town in Turkey on a hot afternoon, you might find everyone walking toward the town square where the camels are going to fight.

Both camels are males. Their owners have worked with them for days trying to make them mean and in

*I leaped to the saddle and braced myself.*

*Day begins when the camels are loaded*

*with boxes and bags all lashed on with heavy ropes.*

*Each camel may carry five hundred pounds or more.*

*bad feeling*

a bad <u>mood</u>. They will fight best at certain times of the year, the time when the females are ready to mate. As the day draws near the fighting camels are fed strange foods. They are given spices and hot red peppers. They are also fed a special fighting food made of flour, and finally a drink of a liquid that the camel owners say is magic, and will make their animals try to tear each other apart.

The first camel led into the square is a large white animal. His front feet are tied together to keep him from running away. He is looking all around, swinging his head from side to side. He grumbles and snorts. A cheer rises from the crowd.

Then, from the other side of the dusty square comes another camel. He is somewhat smaller. He is a brown camel, a very mean-looking animal, and his front feet are also tied together. A deep rumble issues from his long throat as he sees the big white camel through bloodshot eyes, and he stumbles as he tries to rush forward.

Quickly the camel owners cut the ropes on their camels' feet. The two giants lunge at each other. Each one tries to get a hold on the other's neck. They have strong jaws filled with broad teeth. Once they clamp down on the neck of their enemy they probably will not <u>let</u> go.

*to allow*

53

Finally one camel is holding the other's neck in his teeth. He will never let go. He paws with his front feet trying to knock the other one to the ground. He pulls and twists with his mouth. Slowly, very slowly, the loser is forced to the ground. The camel that killed him backs away. Some governments have not yet managed to stop these cruel camel fights.

One day many years ago, before the war between the states, a colonel in the United States Army sat at his desk looking at a map of the southwestern United States. He had a big problem. In those days the Army was building forts in lonely places on the frontier. Some of these were in desert country. The big problem was how to haul supplies to the soldiers across the desert. There still were no trains there. Trucks had not even been invented. But the colonel had an idea. He felt very good about this plan. Why had he not thought of it before? This was desert country and there was an animal made to order for deserts. If camels work in Asia and Africa, why would they not work well in Texas too?

Before long an army officer was on a ship sailing off to Asia to buy some camels. It was May, 1856 when he returned. He brought back thirty-four healthy camels, and he was very happy with them.

*How much work one of these animals can do depends on how well it is fed and watered, how hot the weather, and how fast the march.*

*Even camels do not like camels. They often fight and bite when they come close to each other.*

But not everyone was happy to see the camels. American soldiers had only worked with mules and horses. They liked mules and horses. Mules and horses would listen to reason. Camels wanted everything their own way. The camels tried to kick and bite the soldiers. They even tried to spit on them.

In addition, the camels scared all the mules and horses. They caused horses to run away with wagons. When the soldiers took their strings of camels into town, horses that saw the camels coming pitched and bucked until they threw their riders into the dusty streets.

This got so bad that Brownsville, Texas, passed a law against anyone leading a camel down one of its streets. Later Nevada passed a law against camels anywhere on its roads. Officials said anyone bringing his camel onto a Nevada highway would be put into jail for thirty days.

Years passed. There was less and less work for the camels and fewer people who wanted them around at all. Some camels worked for a while hauling the mail and other goods over rough trails.

One job some of these camels had was helping in the surveying of the rugged border country between California and Arizona. The Army was asked to supply four of its best camels to haul the surveyor's equipment. The four camels were chosen. They were fine

Army camels. But one, named "Toule," had big teeth and strong jaws and wanted to bite anything that got within reach. She was even meaner than most other camels.

Another of the camels was named "Said," and Said made a bad mistake one day; she came too close to Toule. Before Said knew what was happening, Toule reached out and grabbed Said. She bit so hard that Said died. From then on Toule had to help carry Said's load, which seems fair enough.

But Said was honored posthumously. Her bones were shipped off to the Smithsonian Institution in Washington, D.C. And that is all that is left of the camels that were brought to America to work in the deserts.

Wherever he is, a camel is probably happiest when people leave him alone. Then he can do his camel things. He can look for a drink of water. He can practice swatting flies. He can eat a few thorn bushes and build up new fat in that strange hump on his back. He can get ready to live through the next sand storm or long, dry march.

If he thought about it, the camel might feel proud of himself. His talents are many. His history is long and noble. No other animal anyplace could do his work as well. He is the real "ship of the desert."

GEORGE LAYCOCK has written more than twenty books on natural history and conservation. He has also written several hundred articles for many national magazines, including *Field and Stream, Sports Illustrated, Audubon, Better Homes and Gardens,* and *Boys' Life.* When he writes of animals and the outdoors, he deals with subjects of life-long interest. He is a native of Ohio, and holds a degree in wildlife management from the Ohio State University. He has traveled and camped widely, gathering information and taking pictures for his articles and books.